Who is this book for?

Welcome to the world of financial markets trading! This comprehensive guide, presented in the form of a book, is designed for those who are eager to learn about the intricacies of trading and the opportunities it provides. Whether you are a seasoned investor or an aspiring trader, this guide is tailored to fit your needs and elevate your skills to the next level.

With the vast and complex world of financial markets, it's imperative to have a thorough understanding of the underlying principles and techniques of trading. The guide will take you through the fundamental concepts of trading, starting with an introduction to the various financial instruments, trading styles, and intricacies of market analysis.

The guide will provide you with the essential knowledge to build and implement successful trading strategies, explore different trading platforms and tools, and equip you with the skills to manage risk effectively. Additionally, you will be introduced to the concept of leverage and the importance of margin trading.

Here is one of the most recent readers:

Let's meet Jenny, a young graduate who has always been fascinated by the financial markets. Jenny has a degree in finance, but he never felt confident enough to start trading. He felt he needed guidance on how to get started, what to look out for, and how to make profitable trades. He stumbled upon this book and decided to give it a shot.

After reading the book, Jenny was amazed at how much he had learned about the different markets, how they function, and what factors impact them. He also learned about the different trading strategies and how to apply them effectively.

Jenny's most significant takeaway from the book was the emphasis on risk management. He learned how to manage his risks and avoid common pitfalls many traders face. He also discovered the importance of having a trading plan and sticking to it.

Jenny started trading with a small account and was initially nervous. But armed with the knowledge he gained from the book, he was able to make consistent profits. He was amazed at how quickly his account grew, and he felt a sense of accomplishment knowing that he was doing something he had always wanted to do.

As Jenny continued to trade, he found he was becoming more confident and making better trades. He was also able to identify potential risks and avoid them. Jenny felt like he had found his calling, and he was excited about what he could achieve with his trading career.

The guide is designed to cater to a wide range of readers, from novice to experienced traders, and is structured to provide a step-by-step approach to learning. The aim is to empower readers to trade with confidence, make informed decisions, and achieve financial success.

The opportunities that will open for readers who master the content of this guide are limitless. Whether it's supplementing your income, building a long-term investment portfolio, or becoming a professional trader, this guide will provide you with the knowledge and tools to achieve your financial goals.

So, get ready to embark on a journey of discovery and unlock the potential of financial markets trading with this comprehensive guide!

In addition to providing a comprehensive guide to financial markets trading, we have included a quiz at the end of the book to test your knowledge and help reinforce the concepts you have learned. The quiz is designed to be challenging but fair, covering a range of topics from the fundamentals of trading to more advanced strategies and techniques. By taking the quiz, you can assess your understanding of the material and identify areas where you may need further study or practice. Ultimately, our goal is to provide you with the tools and knowledge necessary to succeed as a trader, and the quiz is just one way we are committed to helping you achieve your goals.

What is a market?

In economics, a market is a mechanism through which buyers and sellers interact to exchange goods or services. It refers to a physical or virtual space where buyers and sellers come together to engage in trade.

In a market, buyers and sellers negotiate the price and quantity of goods or services being exchanged based on supply and demand. In a free market, prices are determined by the forces of supply and demand, and buyers and sellers are free to make their own decisions without any external interference.

Markets can take many different forms, such as physical marketplaces like farmers' markets, or online marketplaces like eBay or Amazon. They can also refer to specific industries or asset classes, such as the stock market or the real estate market.

Understanding how markets work is essential for anyone interested in trading or investing in financial markets, as it provides insights into the behavior of prices and how they are influenced by various factors, such as economic indicators, news events, and geopolitical developments.

What types of markets exist?

There are several types of markets, each with its characteristics and participants. Here are some of the most common types of markets:

1. Equity market: This refers to the market for stocks, which represent ownership in a company. The equity market is also known as the stock market, and it is a key component of the financial system.
2. Bond market: This is the market for fixed-income securities, such as government and corporate bonds. The bond market is an important source of financing for governments and corporations.
3. Foreign exchange market: Also known as the forex market, this is the market for trading currencies. It is the largest financial market in the world and is used by governments, banks, and corporations to manage their exposure to foreign currencies.

4. Commodity market: This is the market for trading physical commodities such as gold, oil, and agricultural products. The commodity market is used by producers and consumers to manage price risk.
5. Derivatives market: This is the market for financial instruments whose value is derived from an underlying asset or benchmark. Examples of derivatives include options, futures, and swaps.
6. Real estate market: This is the market for buying and selling real estate, including residential and commercial properties.
7. Auction market: This is a market where buyers and sellers come together to trade goods or services through a bidding process.

Understanding the different types of markets is important for investors and traders as it helps them identify opportunities and manage risk. Each market has its unique characteristics, and it is important to understand these before entering into any trade.

What other than financial markets exist?

Many types of markets exist beyond financial markets. Here are some examples:

1. Consumer goods market: This refers to the market for physical goods that are produced and sold to end consumers. Examples include clothing, electronics, and food.
2. Services market: This refers to the market for intangible services that are provided to consumers. Examples include healthcare, education, and transportation.

3. Labor market: This refers to the market for jobs and employment. Job seekers and employers come together to negotiate terms of employment such as wages and benefits.
4. Real estate market: This market involves buying, selling, and renting land, buildings, and other types of real estate.
5. Agricultural market: This refers to the market for agricultural products, including crops, livestock, and dairy.
6. Energy market: This market involves the production, distribution, and consumption of energy resources such as oil, gas, and electricity.
7. Technology market: This market involves the buying and selling of technological products and services, such as software, hardware, and telecommunications.
8. Art market: This market involves the buying and selling of works of art, including paintings, sculptures, and other forms of visual art.

Understanding the various markets that exist beyond financial markets is important as it can help individuals and businesses make informed decisions about where to invest their time, money, and resources.

Here are three major types of financial markets:

1. Stock market: A stock market is where publicly traded companies issue shares that can be bought and sold by investors. Stock prices are determined by supply and demand, and are influenced by various factors such as company performance, economic indicators, and investor sentiment.
2. Bond market: A bond market is where companies, governments, and other entities issue bonds that can be bought and sold by investors. Bonds are debt securities that pay fixed or variable interest to investors, and their prices are influenced by factors such as interest rates, credit risk, and inflation expectations.
3. Foreign exchange market: The foreign exchange (Forex) market is where currencies are bought and sold by individuals, businesses, and governments. It is the largest financial market in the world, and its prices are determined by supply and demand for different currencies, as well as various economic and geopolitical factors.

Introduction to Trading

Trading is the act of buying and selling financial instruments, such as stocks, bonds, currencies, and commodities, intending to make a profit. It has been around for centuries and has evolved. Today, trading is done primarily through electronic platforms, which have made it more accessible than ever before.

To be a successful trader, you need to understand some key terms and concepts. Securities, for example, are financial instruments that can be traded, such as stocks, bonds, and options. Investing is the act of putting money into something with the expectation of making a profit. Risk refers to the possibility of losing money in a trade, while the return is the potential profit.

Finally, it's important to understand the role that financial markets play in the global economy. The stock market, for example, is a way for companies to raise capital by selling shares to the public. The forex market, on the other hand, is where currencies are traded, and it plays a crucial role in international trade and investment.

Understanding the Markets

To be a successful trader, you need to understand the markets you're trading in. Financial markets can generally be divided into three main types: security, commodity, and forex. While they have some similarities, there are also significant differences between them. Each market operates in its unique way, with its unique characteristics and features.

The security market is the most well-known of the three. It includes stocks and bonds, which are traded on exchanges such as the New York Stock Exchange (NYSE) and NASDAQ. When you purchase a stock, you are buying a small ownership stake in a company. As a result, your share's value is determined by the company's financial performance and future prospects. On the other hand, bonds represent a debt that companies or governments take on, which they promise to pay back over time with interest.

Commodity markets deal with physical goods such as agricultural products, metals, and energy resources. Commodity prices are influenced by supply and demand, just like stocks and bonds. For instance, if there is a shortage of oil due to a natural disaster or geopolitical tensions, oil prices will rise. Investors in commodity markets can either invest in futures contracts or in commodity ETFs (Exchange-Traded Funds) that track the price of commodities.

The foreign exchange (forex) market is where currency trading takes place. Forex traders buy and sell currencies, attempting to profit from changes in exchange rates.

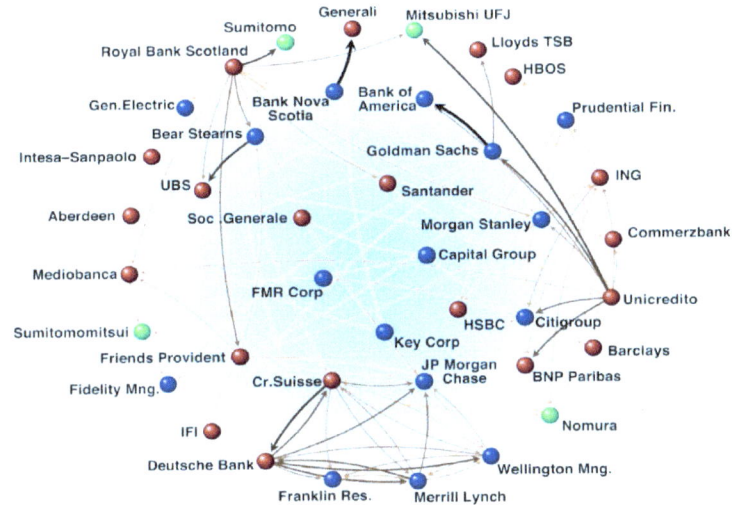

Forex, or foreign exchange or currency trading, is the world's largest and most liquid market, with daily trading volumes of over $6 trillion. It involves buying and selling currencies from different countries to make a profit.

Imagine you are going on vacation to Europe from the United States. It would help if you exchanged US dollars for euros while there. The exchange rate between the two currencies will determine how many euros you will receive for your dollars.

Imagine you have European friends who want to buy new cars from the United States. They must exchange their euros for US dollars to pay for the vehicles. Again, the exchange rate will determine how many dollars they must pay for the car.

This is where forex trading comes in. Traders can buy and sell currencies based on their market analysis and economic factors that may impact the exchange rates.

For example, if a trader believes that the US economy is growing faster than the European economy, they may decide to buy US dollars and sell euros.

Forex trading is accessible to individuals, banks, corporations, and governments. It is open 24 hours a day, five days a week, and is a highly liquid market. Traders can use various trading strategies and tools to analyse the market and make informed decisions about when to buy and sell currencies.

In summary, forex trading involves the buying and selling of currencies to make a profit. It is a dynamic and exciting market accessible to anyone with an internet connection and a willingness to learn.

The cryptocurrency market has become a popular alternative to the forex market, with digital currencies such as Bitcoin, Ethereum, and Litecoin being traded on exchanges. While both forex and cryptocurrencies are decentralized markets, their underlying technology, regulatory frameworks, and risk profiles differ.

Overall, each financial market serves a different purpose and attracts different types of investors. Understanding the characteristics and nuances of each market is critical for successful investing. By diversifying their portfolio across different financial markets, investors can reduce their risk exposure and increase their chances of generating long-term returns.

To succeed in any of these markets, you need to understand the factors that can impact market prices. Economic indicators, such as GDP and inflation, can have a significant impact, as can geopolitical events, such as wars and elections. Company news, such as earnings reports and product launches, can also impact stock prices.

Before choosing a market and business, it is important to consider the following characteristics:

1. Supply and demand price dependence

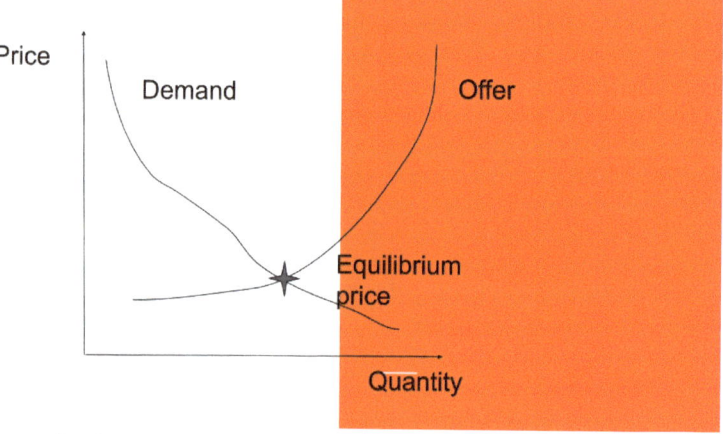

Understanding the supply and demand of the market is crucial for any business, as it affects the prices of goods and services. A market with high demand and low supply may lead to higher prices, while a market with low demand and high supply may lead to lower prices.

2. Liquidity

Liquidity refers to the ease with which assets can be bought or sold without affecting the price. A liquid market provides more opportunities to buy and sell and typically has lower transaction costs.
In this image, which of the assets is the most liquid?

3. Market size

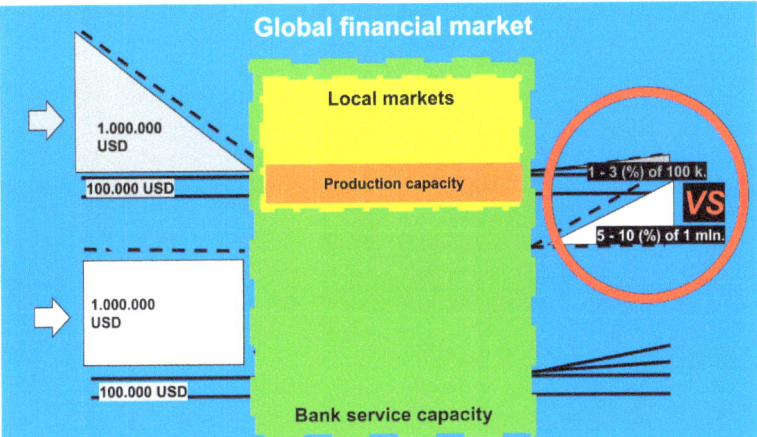

The size of the market can impact a business in terms of the potential customer base and competition. A larger market may have more customers but also more competition, while a smaller market may have fewer customers but also less competition.

4. Manipulation:

Some markets may be prone to manipulation, such as insider trading or market manipulation by larger players.
If someone wishes to push the price up, they should control at least 1/3 of the market's capital to get it done.

It is important to choose a market that is regulated and has measures in place to prevent manipulation. Generally, smaller markets are more susceptible to price manipulation than larger markets. This is because smaller markets have fewer participants, and the actions of a single participant can have a greater impact on the market as a whole. Additionally, smaller markets often have less liquidity, which can make it easier for a manipulator to move prices in their desired direction.

However, it is important to note that even larger markets can be subject to price manipulation, particularly in instances where a single participant or group of participants has a significant amount of influence or control over the market.

5. Flexibility
Flexibility is important when choosing a business type because it allows for greater adaptability and agility in responding to changing market conditions,

customer demands, and technological advancements. For example, online trading offers the flexibility to work from anywhere with an internet connection, allowing traders to monitor and trade financial markets from the comfort of their homes or while traveling.

Similarly, a production factory with a flexible manufacturing system can quickly adjust production schedules and product lines in response to changes in demand or supply chain disruptions. This flexibility helps businesses to optimize operations and increase profitability while minimizing risk and exposure.

In contrast, businesses with rigid structures and processes may struggle to respond effectively to changes in the market or adapt to new technologies, potentially resulting in missed opportunities or even failure. Therefore, flexibility is an important consideration when choosing a business type. Different markets require different resources, such as equipment, technology, or specialised skills. It is important to consider these requirements when choosing a market.

Investment and reinvestment thresholds
Starting and running a business in a market often requires significant investments of capital. It is important to consider the investment and reinvestment thresholds of a market when deciding whether it is viable for a business.

Closing business threshold
It is important to consider the costs and ease of closing a business in a market. Some markets may have high barriers to exit or high costs associated with closing a business.

6. Geolocation
Geolocation is essential for choosing a business type because it can impact the availability of resources and market conditions that can affect the success of a business. For example, suppose a company is located in an area with a high demand for its products or services; it may be more profitable to focus on retail sales or production at a factory to meet the demand. On the other hand, if the business is located in an area with a thriving stock market or a large number of forex traders, it may be more advantageous to invest in those markets to maximize profits.

Furthermore, geolocation can also impact the regulatory environment that a business operates in. Countries and regions may have different laws and regulations regarding trading activities, taxes, and other business-related activities. This can affect the costs and risks associated with operating in a particular market and influence a business's decision to enter or exit a market.

In summary, geolocation is an essential factor in choosing a business type because it can affect the availability of resources, market conditions, and regulatory environment, which can impact the profitability and success of a business.

7. Regulations
Markets are regulated by different government agencies, and it is important to understand the regulations that apply to a specific market. Regulations can impact the costs, operations, and compliance requirements of a business.

8. Working hours

The working hours of a market can impact a business in terms of its ability to operate efficiently and effectively. It is important to consider the working hours of a market and how they align with the needs of the business.

The forex market is open 24 hours a day, 5 days a week, which means that trading can take place at any time. However, there are certain periods of time when the market is more active and when trading volumes are higher. These periods are known as trading sessions and they are generally divided into three main sessions:

1. Asian session: The Asian trading session begins at 10:00 PM GMT on Sunday and ends at 9:00 AM GMT on Monday. This session is dominated by the markets of Japan, China, Australia, and New Zealand.
2. European session: The European trading session starts at 7:00 AM GMT and ends at 4:00 PM GMT. This session is dominated by the markets of London, Frankfurt, and Paris.
3. US session: The US trading session starts at 12:00 PM GMT and ends at 9:00 PM GMT. This session is dominated by the markets of New York, Chicago, and Los Angeles.

It is worth noting that there is some overlap between these sessions. For example, the European and US sessions overlap for a few hours, which can lead to increased volatility and trading activity during that time. Additionally, there are some regional sessions that take place outside of these main sessions, such as the Tokyo and Sydney sessions. Understanding the trading sessions can be useful for traders as it can help them to identify the best times to trade based on their trading strategy and the currencies they are trading.

Let's analyse the difference between 4 businesses and their market types
Table 1.

Characteristics	Forex Trading	IKEA Stocks Trading	Furniture Sales in Distribution	Furniture Factory
Supply and Demand	High	Medium	Medium	Medium
Liquidity	High	High	Medium	Low
Market Size	Very High	High	High	Medium
Manipulation	Very Low	Low	High	High
Resources Needed to Operate	Low	Low	Medium	High
Investment and Reinvestment	High	High	Medium	High
Closing Business Threshold	Low	Low	High	High

Geolocation	Anywhere	Anywhere	Local	Local
Regulations	Medium	High	High	High
Working Hours	24/5	09:00-17:30	09:00-18:00	24/5
Risks	High	Medium	Medium	High

According to table 1, we can make some general observations:

- Forex trading has high liquidity and a large market size, but is subject to high manipulation risks and requires significant resources to operate effectively.
- Ikea stocks trading has medium liquidity and market size, with low manipulation risks and lower resource requirements compared to forex trading.
- Furniture sales in distribution may have lower liquidity and market size compared to the other businesses, but have low manipulation risks and lower investment and reinvestment thresholds. However, it may require a physical location and significant closing business thresholds.
- Furniture factory has a lower liquidity and market size compared to forex trading and Ikea stocks trading, but may have lower manipulation risks and may not require as high of investment and reinvestment thresholds as forex trading.

Ultimately, Forex trading has the best parameters for profitable business, however, the "best" business type will depend on an individual or company's specific goals, resources, and risk tolerance.

The highest risk is also in forex trading, mainly because of high volatility, but at the same time, this is one of the main causes of the highest profitability. There are no miracles. What gives more, may take more.

What does the forex look like?

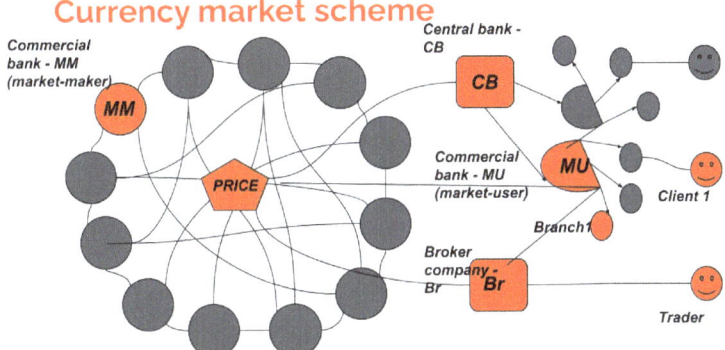

Who are the forex participants?

Forex participants are individuals, institutions, and entities that participate in the foreign exchange market, also known as the forex market. The forex market is a global decentralised market for the trading of currencies, where buyers and sellers exchange one currency for another at an agreed-upon price.

There are several types of forex participants. Each has different goals and objectives when participating in the foreign exchange market. Here are some of the common goals for each of the forex participants:

Commercial banks (Market makers)

These are the primary participants in the forex market. Banks buy and sell currencies on behalf of their clients and for their accounts.

Commercial banks aim to earn a profit by buying and selling currencies for their clients and for their accounts. They also participate in the forex market to manage their currency exposures.

Central banks

Central banks participate in the forex market to manage their country's currency reserves, stabilise their currency's value, and influence their economy's monetary policy.

Central banks participate in the forex market to manage their country's currency reserves, stabilize their currency's value, and influence their economy's monetary policy.

Hedge funds

Hedge funds trade in the forex market to profit from changes in currency exchange rates.
Hedge funds trade in the forex market to profit from changes in currency exchange rates. They typically use leverage to amplify their returns.

International corporations

International corporations participate in the forex market to exchange currencies for their international business operations.

Retail forex traders

Individuals who trade currencies through online forex brokers are known as retail forex traders.

Some use trading as the primary job, others as part-time or additional to the main one. Their goal is to make profits from currency price movements.

Tourists and other international travelers

Tourists are considered forex participants because when they travel to another country, they typically exchange their domestic currency for their local currency. For example, if a tourist from the United Kingdom travels to France, they must exchange GB pounds for euros to spend money while in France.

Financial markets trading principles and standards

Trading volumes and lots

Imagine walking into a bustling marketplace, with vendors shouting out their prices and eager buyers haggling over the best deals. This is the world of financial markets, where millions of traders from around the globe come together to buy and sell a vast array of financial instruments, such as stocks, commodities, crypto, and most importantly, currencies.

One of the most important metrics that traders and investors use to gauge the activity and liquidity of these markets is the trading volume. This refers to the total number of shares, contracts, or lots that are bought and sold in a given period, typically measured in a day, a week, or a month. The higher the trading volume, the more active and dynamic the market is.

But what is a trading lot? In simple terms, a lot is a standardized unit of measurement that represents the size of a trade. In the world of forex trading, a standard lot is equal to 100,000 units of the base currency, which is the first currency listed in a currency pair. For example, in the EUR/USD pair, the euro is the base currency, so one standard lot of this pair would be 100,000 euros.

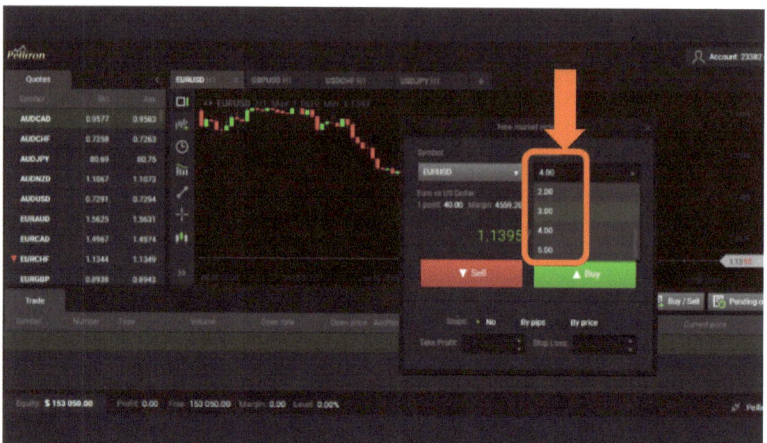

However, not all traders have the same amount of capital to trade with, and not all markets have the same lot sizes. For instance, in the stock market, a lot typically represents 100 shares of a particular stock. In the commodities market, the lot size can vary depending on the specific commodity being traded.

Overall, understanding trading volumes and lot sizes is essential for anyone looking to trade in financial markets, especially forex. By keeping an eye on trading volumes and lot sizes, traders can stay informed about the market activity and make more informed decisions about their trades.

Marginal trading

Margin trading is a sophisticated investment technique that allows traders to amplify their buying power by borrowing funds from a broker to open larger positions than their capital would allow. In essence, margin trading enables traders to multiply their potential profits (or losses) by leveraging their investments.

The concept of margin trading has been around for centuries, dating back to the days when stockbrokers would lend money to wealthy investors to buy shares on credit. However, it wasn't until the late 19th century that margin trading became widely available to the general public. Today, margin trading is a popular practice among traders in various financial markets, including the forex market.

A scheme of a marginal trading system typically involves three key elements. These include:

Margin = pledge => *n*

Leverage = multiplier => *n : x*n*

Balance - available funds => *x*n*

Margin: The margin is the amount of money the trader must deposit to open a position using leverage. The margin is typically a percentage of the total position size and is used to cover any potential losses.

Leverage: Marginal trading allows traders to use leverage, meaning they can trade larger positions than they could with their available funds. The leverage is provided by the broker, who lends the trader the necessary funds to open the position.

Balance: Funds available for trading.

The impact of margin trading on traders can be significant, as it allows them to access greater amounts of capital than they would otherwise be able to afford. This can result in greater profits if the trader's positions perform well, but it can also lead to substantial losses if the positions move against them.

For traders in the forex market, margin trading can be particularly attractive due to the available high levels of leverage. The forex market is known for its high liquidity and volatility, which can result in significant price movements in short periods. With margin trading, traders can take advantage of these movements by opening large positions with relatively small amounts of capital.

However, it's important to note that margin trading can also be risky, as it magnifies both profits and losses. Traders who use margin trading must be careful to manage their risk appropriately and use stop-loss orders to limit their potential losses. Overall, margin trading can be a powerful tool for experienced traders who are willing to take on the associated risks.

!!! The leverage should be chosen according to trading strategy and business plan.

Spread and prices

Imagine you are a tourist who is planning a trip to Europe and you need to exchange your currency (let's say US dollars) for euros. You walk into a currency exchange office and you notice that they display two different prices for EUR/USD: the bid price and the ask price.

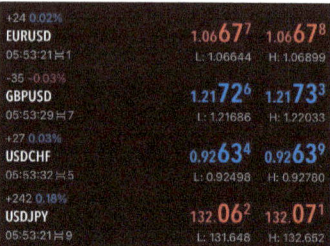

The bid price is the price at which the exchange office is willing to buy your US dollars in exchange for euros. The ask price, on the other hand, is the price at which the exchange office is willing to sell euros in exchange for your US dollars.

Let's say the exchange office is quoting a bid price of 1.1800 and an ask price of 1.2000 for EUR/USD. This means that if you want to sell US dollars and buy euros, the exchange office will buy your US dollars at a rate of 1.1800 euros per dollar. Conversely, if you want to buy euros and sell US dollars, the exchange office will sell you euros at a rate of 1.2000 euros per dollar.

The difference between the bid and ask prices is known as the spread, and it represents the profit margin for the exchange office. In this example, the spread is 0.0200, or 200 pips. This means that if you buy euros at the ask price of 1.2000 and then immediately sell them back to the exchange office at the bid price of 1.1800, you would incur a loss of 200 pips.

So, if you exchange $1000 for euros at the ask price of 1.2000, you would receive €833.33. If you immediately exchange those euros back to US dollars at the bid price of 1.1800, you would receive $981.13. In this case, you would have incurred a loss of $18.87 due to the spread.

Both the tourist and the exchange office have an interest in the deal. The tourist wants to get the best possible exchange rate and minimize the cost of exchanging money. On the other hand, the exchange office wants to make a profit on the transaction. The spread represents the compromise between these two interests. The exchange office needs to offer a rate that is attractive enough to the tourist while still generating a profit for the business.

Overall, understanding the bid and ask prices and the spread is essential for anyone who needs to exchange currency. By shopping around and comparing exchange rates from different exchange offices, tourists can get the best possible rate and minimize the cost of exchanging money.

Let's assume that the tourist exchanged $1000 for euros at the ask price of 1.2000 and received €833.33. After a few days, the exchange rate changed in the tourist's favor, and the new quote is a bid price of 1.1900 and an ask price of 1.2100 for EUR/USD.

If the tourist decided to exchange the euros back to US dollars at the bid price of 1.1900, they would receive $988.12. This means that they would have made a profit of $7.99 ($988.12 - $981.13) on the initial exchange, after taking into account the spread.

It's important to note that exchange rates are constantly fluctuating, and for nonprofessionals, it's impossible to predict exactly how they will change in the future. However, if the tourist was able to take advantage of a favourable exchange rate and make a profit, they would have effectively reduced the cost of their trip by minimising the cost of exchanging money.

There are several key differences between a tourist and a professional forex trader in this situation.

Firstly, a professional forex trader would likely have access to more sophisticated tools and analysis techniques than a tourist. They may use technical analysis, fundamental analysis, or a combination of both to predict future exchange rate movements and identify profitable trading opportunities.

Secondly, a professional forex trader would be trading with larger amounts of money and would likely have a more robust risk management strategy in place. They would be aware of the potential risks of exchange rate fluctuations and would take steps to minimize their exposure to these risks, such as by using stop-loss orders or hedging their positions.

Thirdly, a professional forex trader would be operating with a different set of goals than a tourist. While a tourist is primarily concerned with getting the best possible exchange rate to minimize the cost of their trip, a professional forex trader is focused on generating profits from trading forex. Their goal is to buy currencies when they are undervalued and sell them when they are overvalued, to make a profit on the difference in exchange rates.

Overall, the differences between a tourist and a professional forex trader lie in their access to resources, their risk management strategies, and their goals. While a tourist is looking for a good exchange rate to minimize costs, a professional trader is focused on generating profits through trading forex.

A great point to add! Professional forex traders typically trade in much larger volumes than tourists, which means that they can negotiate better exchange rates and benefit from smaller spreads.

For example, a professional forex trader may be able to negotiate an exchange rate of 1.2000 (bid) | 1.2005 (ask) for a trade worth $10 million, while a tourist may only be able to get an exchange rate of 1.8000 (bid) | 1.2000 (ask) for a trade worth $1,000. This small difference in the exchange rate can have a significant impact on the profits made from the trade.

In addition, professional forex traders often have access to institutional trading platforms that offer more favourable pricing and tighter spreads. These platforms are designed for high-volume trading and can offer significant cost savings compared to retail trading platforms.

Overall, the ability to negotiate better exchange rates and benefit from smaller spreads allows professional forex traders to generate larger profits from their trades.

Direct and indirect currency pairs

The foreign exchange market, or Forex, is the largest and most liquid market in the world, with over $6 trillion traded daily. The Forex market allows for the exchange of currencies from all over the world, with the most commonly traded currencies being known as the "major" currencies.

Five major currencies are traded in the Forex market: the US dollar (USD), the euro (EUR), the Japanese yen (JPY), the British pound (GBP) and the Swiss franc (CHF). These currencies are often paired with each other, creating various currency pairs that are traded in the Forex market:

EUR/USD

GBP/USD

USD/JPY

USD/CHF.

When trading Forex, currency pairs are quoted using a bid-ask spread. The bid price is the price at which a trader can sell a currency pair, while the ask price is the price at which a trader can buy a currency pair. The difference between the bid and ask price is known as the spread, and it represents the cost of trading Forex.

There are two main types of currency quotes: direct quotes and indirect quotes. Direct quotes are quoted in terms of a currency's value concerning the US dollar. For example, a direct quote for the EUR/USD currency pair might be 1.2000, which means that one euro is worth 1.2000 US dollars. Indirect quotes, on the other hand, are quoted in terms of a currency's value concerning another currency. For example, an indirect quote for the USD/JPY currency pair might be 133.70, which means that one dollar is worth 133.70 Japanese yen. It is considered indirect because after the deal is closed, the income is calculated in USD, meaning that one more operation is needed for converting the yen to the dollar.

Another type of currency quote is a cross currency quote, which represents the exchange rate between two currencies that are not the US dollar. For example, a cross currency quote for the EUR/JPY currency pair might be 143.09, which means that one euro is worth 143.09 Japanese yen.

Overall, understanding the main currencies traded, the main quotes, and their types are essential for any forex trader. By staying informed about exchange rates and trends in the forex market, traders can make more informed trading decisions and maximise their profits.

Deal processing example

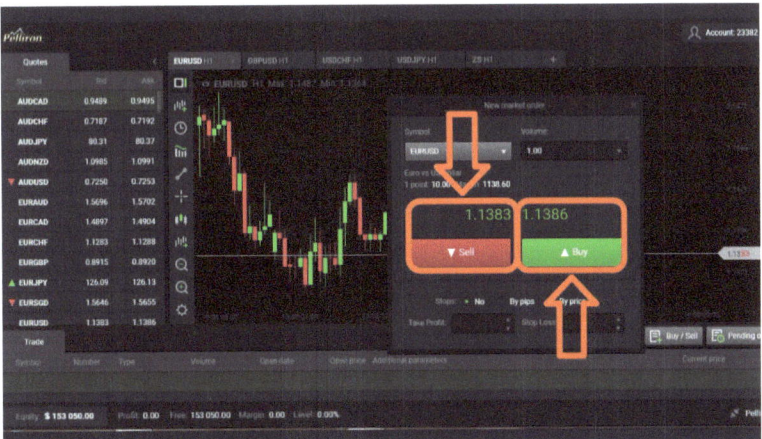

Assuming we want to buy 1 lot of EUR/USD at the current bid/ask price of 1.0704/1.0707, here's how the calculation works:

1. Lot size: 1 lot
2. Base currency: EUR
3. Quote currency: USD
4. Bid price: 1.0704
5. Ask price: 1.0707

To calculate the required margin for a 1:100 leverage, we first need to calculate the notional value of the trade:

Notional value = lot size * contract size * ask price

The contract size for EUR/USD = 100,000

Notional value = 1 * 100,000 * 1.0707 = 107,070 USD

Now, to calculate the required margin, we use the leverage formula:

Required margin = notional value/leverage

Required margin = 107,070 / 100 = 1,070.70 USD

So the trader would need to have at least 1,070.70 USD in their trading account to open this trade with a 1:100 leverage.

Assuming the next day the price of EUR/USD increased to 1.0775/1.0778 and the trader decides to close the trade, here's how the income statement would look like:

Profit/Loss = (closing price - opening price) * lot size * lots quantity

Pip value for EUR/USD = 0.0001 (since it's a 4-decimal currency pair)

Opening price = 1.0707

Closing price = 1.0775

Profit/Loss = (1.0775 - 1.0707) * 100,000 * 1 = 680 USD

So the trader would have made a profit of 680 USD on this trade. The income statement would look like this:

Revenue (selling price) = 107,750 USD

Cost (buying price) = 107,070 USD

Profit = 680 USD

Overall, the trader would have earned a profit of 680 USD on this trade.

The price changed by 68 pips, meaning the minimal price deviation of 1 pip = 0.0001 = 10 USD for 1 lot direct quote.

Example with an indirect quote:

Assuming we want to sell 1 lot of USD/JPY at the current bid/ask price of 133.70/133.73, here's how the calculation works:

1. Lot size: 1 lot
2. Base currency: USD
3. Quote currency: JPY
4. Bid price: 133.70
5. Ask price: 133.73

To calculate the required margin for a 1:100 leverage, we first need to calculate the notional value of the trade:

Notional value = lot size * contract size * bid price

The contract size for USD/JPY = 100,000

Notional value = 1 * 100,000 * 133.70 = 13,370,000 JPY

Required margin = 1,000 USD

So the trader would need to have at least 1,000 USD in their trading account to open this trade with a 1:100 leverage.

Assuming the next day the price of USD/JPY increased to 134.15/134.18 and the trader decides to close the trade, here's how the income statement would look like:

Profit/Loss = (opening price - closing price) * lot size * lots quantity / closing price

Pip value for USD/JPY = 0.01 (since it's a 2-decimal currency pair)

Opening price = 133.70

Closing price = 134.18

Profit/Loss = (133.70 - 134.18) * 100,000 * 1 / 134.18 = (357.72) USD loss

So the trader would have incurred a loss of 45 USD on this trade. The income statement would look like this:

Revenue (selling price) = 13,370,000 JPY (converted to USD using the USD/JPY exchange rate)

Cost (buying price) = 13,418,000 JPY (converted to USD using the USD/JPY exchange rate)

Profit/Loss = (357.72) USD (loss)

Overall, the trader would have incurred a loss of 357.72 USD on this trade.

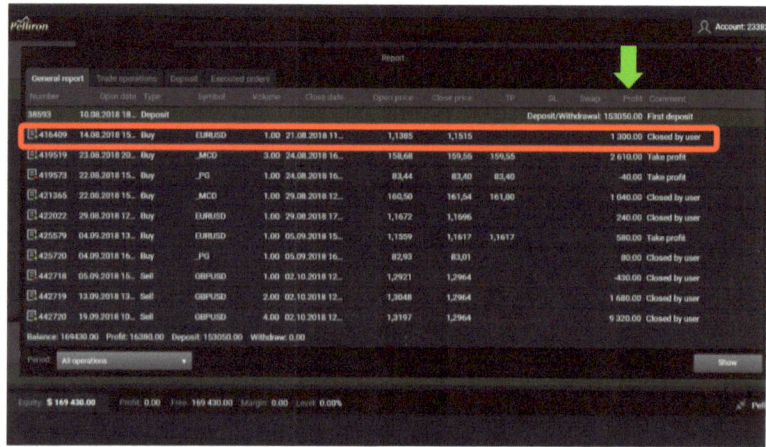

Traders do not calculate these results, as the trading platform is calculating them. However, a professional trader should know how the results appear.

Fundamental Analysis - Digging Deeper

Have you ever wondered what separates successful forex traders from the rest?

How do they know when to buy and sell currencies?

While there are various strategies and techniques, one key aspect that successful traders swear by is fundamental analysis.

Fundamental analysis is a method of analyzing the financial health of a country's economy to evaluate its intrinsic value relative to other currencies. The objective is to determine whether a currency is overvalued or undervalued relative to its economic prospects.

So, what does fundamental analysis entail in the forex markets?

Let's dive in.

Understanding Economic Indicators

At the heart of fundamental analysis in forex lies the economic indicators of a country. These indicators provide an overview of the country's economic performance and position. There are various economic indicators, including GDP, inflation rate, interest rate, trade balance, and many more.

GDP reflects the country's economic output over a specific period, usually a quarter or a year. It shows whether the country's economy is growing or contracting.

The inflation rate reflects the rate at which prices of goods and services are increasing in the country. It provides insight into the country's monetary policy and its impact on the economy.

The interest rate reflects the rate at which the central bank lends money to commercial banks. It affects the country's borrowing and lending rates, which, in turn, affects the economy's growth.

As a forex trader, you know that keeping a keen eye on central bank interest rates can lead to profitable opportunities. The central bank interest rate is the interest rate at which a country's central bank lends money to commercial banks. Its role in influencing borrowing and lending rates within the economy cannot be underestimated. This is why changes in central bank interest rates can have a significant impact on currency prices and present opportunities for traders to make profits.

When the central bank interest rate increases, investors tend to flock to the currency in search of higher returns, which results in a strengthening of its value. On the other hand, a decrease in the interest rate can lead to a decrease in demand for the currency, which can weaken its value. As a trader, you can take advantage of these changes by buying or selling currencies at the right time.

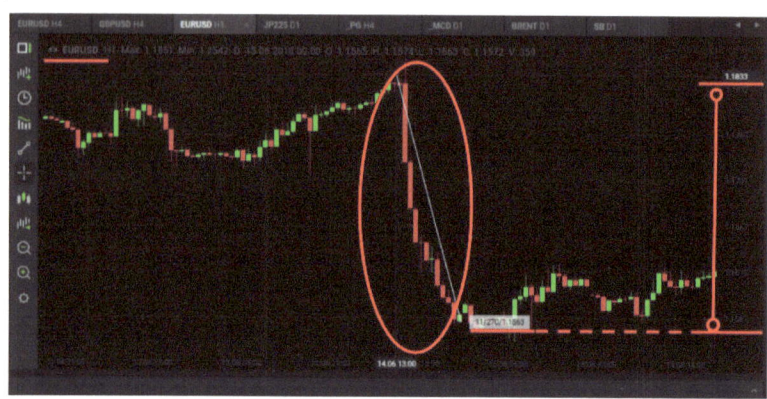

14 June 2018 ECB Press Conference
EUR/USD went down 300 pips in 6 hours

So how fast do these changes happen?

Well, it's worth noting that the impact of a change in central bank interest rates on currency prices can vary based on several factors. The size and timing of the change, market reaction, and overall economic conditions of the country all play a role. However, as a general rule, larger and unexpected changes tend to have a more significant and immediate impact on currency prices. As a result, traders need to keep a close eye on any news or developments that may suggest changes in central bank interest rates.

March 2018 FED increased the rate by 0,25
EUR/USD
USD went down 94 pips in an hour (EUR increased > USD decreased)

The good news is that these changes can present exciting opportunities for traders to make profits. With the right tools and knowledge, traders can make informed decisions and position themselves to benefit from changes in central bank interest rates. So keep your eyes open and stay informed, and you too can make the most of the exciting world of forex trading.

07 September 2018 NFP +54k
EUR/USD
USD went up 110 pips in 10 hours (EUR decreased < USD increased)

Non farm payrolls (NFP) is a monthly report released by the US Bureau of Labor Statistics that provides information on the total number of paid American workers, excluding farm employees, government employees, private household employees, and nonprofit organization employees. It is an important economic indicator that is closely watched by financial markets, economists, and policymakers as it provides insights into the overall health of the US economy and its labor market. The report is based on data collected from a survey of businesses and government agencies and includes information on the unemployment rate, average hourly earnings, and the number of hours worked per week.

05 September 2018 Trade balance (-)
GBP/USD
USD went down 140 pips in 4 hours (GBP increased < USD decreased)

The trade balance reflects the difference between a country's exports and imports. A trade surplus occurs when a country's exports are greater than its imports, while a trade deficit occurs when a country's imports are greater than its exports.

Analysts use various economic indicators and ratios derived from them to evaluate a country's economic performance, such as GDP growth rate, inflation rate, interest rate differential, and trade balance.

Macro and Microeconomic Factors

Apart from economic indicators, the fundamental analysis also considers macro and microeconomic factors that could affect a country's economic performance. These factors include political stability, government policies, natural disasters, and geopolitical tensions.

For instance, a country with stable political conditions is likely to attract more foreign investment, which could strengthen its currency. Similarly, a country that is heavily dependent on a commodity, such as oil, might suffer a decline in its currency value due to fluctuations in commodity prices.

Stock market indexes are essential indicators of the state of the economy. You can trade on them or use them to predict currency price movements.

A stock index, such as the Dow Jones 30, Nasdaq 100, S&P 500, FTSE 100 (Futsi), Dax (30), Nikkei 225, etc., is a measure of the average share price of a particular type or 'weighting' of companies that are included in it.

For example, the Dow Jones 30 Index includes the arithmetic average share price of the 30 largest industrial companies, divided according to a specific formula. Stock market indexes provide a general sense of the state of a country's economy. If the index goes up, these companies' share prices go up, which means they are developing; they also form parts of the country's GDP, i.e., the economy is growing, and the exchange rate is rising.

When the central bank changes its interest rate, the price of the currency goes up, but the stock market indexes go down because new loans for the development of companies are more expensive, which slows down the development of these companies, but at that moment the currency also goes up because some investors get rid of the shares. As the price falls, they sell, but selling is nothing more than exchanging for money, i.e., the demand for money goes up.

When GDP grows - the economy grows, and so does the exchange rate, but gradually, due to the added value, so does inflation. It is needed but at a certain low level. That is why if inflation rises above a certain level, the central bank intervenes and raises the interest rates. And so everything goes round and round in this cycle.

So it is important to understand how to act quickly and in time, which directions currencies, shares, indexes and other financial derivatives are exposed to when economic factors change.

For example:

Above we said that currency did not move much when the rate was changed on September 26, but the stock indexes, for example, the Dow Jones index, fell by 220 points in an hour. As a result, traders made money not on currencies but on the currency itself by selling the stock indexes.

Valuation Techniques

Once an analyst has evaluated the economic indicators and considered the macro and microeconomic factors, the next step is to value the currency. There are various valuation techniques, including purchasing power parity analysis, interest rate parity analysis, and balance of payments analysis.

Purchasing power parity analysis compares the price of goods and services in different countries and adjusts for exchange rate fluctuations. It provides insight into whether a currency is overvalued or undervalued relative to its purchasing power.

Interest rate parity analysis compares the interest rates of different countries and adjusts for exchange rate fluctuations. It provides insight into whether a currency is overvalued or undervalued relative to its interest rate differential.

Balance of payments analysis compares the country's inflows and outflows of foreign currency over a specific period. It provides insight into whether a currency is overvalued or undervalued relative to its balance of payments position.

Conclusion

Fundamental analysis is a crucial tool for forex traders to evaluate a country's economic performance and intrinsic value relative to other currencies. By analyzing the economic indicators, considering macro and microeconomic factors, and using various valuation techniques, traders can make informed trading decisions and increase their chances of success.

As a forex trader, staying up to date with changing information about fundamental analysis is essential to making informed trading decisions. One of the most valuable sources of information for fundamental analysis is economic indicators. These indicators provide important data on a country's economic performance, such as inflation rates, unemployment rates, and GDP growth.

To stay informed about economic indicators and other fundamental analysis news, traders can turn to a range of sources, including their forex broker. Many forex brokers offer their economic calendars that track upcoming releases of economic data, as well as analysis and insights into how these releases may impact currency prices.

For example, popular forex brokers such as IG, Oanda, and Pelliron all provide their clients with access to real-time economic data and analysis. Pelliron, in particular, offers its clients a range of tools and resources to help them stay informed about fundamental analysis, including a comprehensive economic calendar, market news and analysis, and expert insights from its team of analysts.

In addition to utilising the resources provided by their broker, traders can also turn to financial news outlets such as Bloomberg, CNBC, and Reuters for real-time updates on economic data releases and other important news that can impact currency prices. Live market data feeds provided by trading platforms are also a valuable tool for staying informed and monitoring changes in currency prices.

Social media can also be a valuable tool for staying up to date with fundamental analysis news. Following relevant financial experts and analysts on platforms such as Twitter can provide traders with valuable insights and information.

Overall, staying informed about changing information related to fundamental analysis requires a multi-faceted approach. By utilising a combination of resources provided by their broker, financial news outlets, live market data feeds, and social media, traders can stay up to date with the latest developments and make informed trading decisions.

In the next chapter, we'll explore technical analysis, another popular method of analysing forex prices and predicting market trends.

Technical analysis

In addition to fundamental analysis, technical analysis is another approach that many traders use to inform their trading decisions. Technical analysis is the study of historical price and volume data to identify patterns and trends that can help traders predict future price movements.

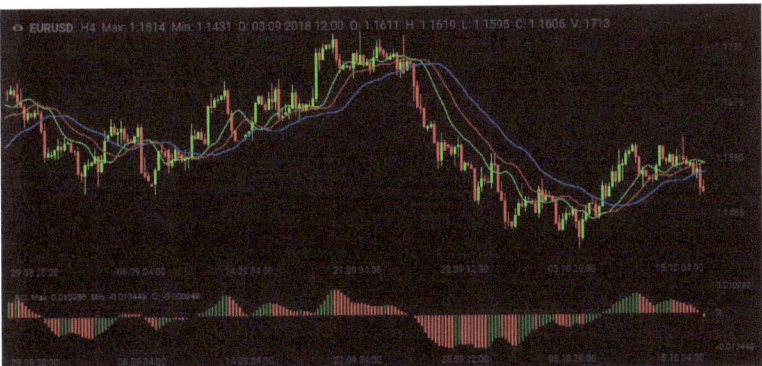

This approach is based on three main postulates or rules, that forex traders (and traders in other markets) should be aware of to effectively use technical analysis.

The first postulate of technical analysis is that the market discounts everything

This means that all known information about a currency pair, including economic and geopolitical events, is reflected in the current price. By analyzing historical price data, forex traders can identify trends and patterns that may help predict future price movements.

For example:

If the unemployment rate goes up, the currency goes down. At the same time, without knowing the news, just by observing the price chart, you can understand the cause-and-effect relationship, not even bother with the news, and sell, since the price is falling.

Charts

A chart is a display of price movements. Previously on special millimeter paper, now in special trading terminals on computer and smartphone screens. Graphs can be characterized by the type of construction and by time intervals.

The type of construction is distinguished:

(a) A line chart, which consists of lines connecting points that represent prices at the end of specific periods

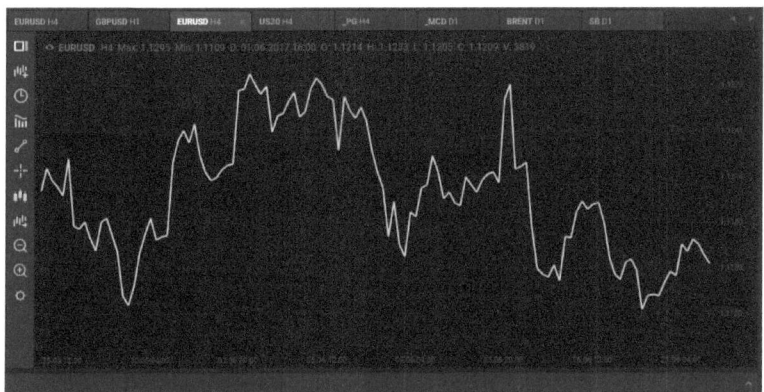

These are the very first graphs. They are usually shown on television news. They are straightforward to understand and show the general trend but inform little about the movements within time intervals. Therefore, they have been replaced by bar and candlestick charts.

(b) The bar chart, which includes four prices: the price at the beginning of the period, the indicator of price change for the whole time interval - the maximum and minimum values, and the price at the end of the time interval (at the last second). This chart type is more informative than the previous one but is tough to perceive. That is why the candlestick chart has replaced it.

(c) Candlestick Chart: This chart type is similar to the bar chart but presents the same information differently. Each candlestick represents one period of time and shows the opening and closing prices and the high and low prices. The candlestick's body is colored differently depending on whether the price closed higher or lower than it opened, making it easier to see trends and patterns in the data.

The last two charts show movements you can't see on a line chart. If, over some time, the price has risen by 100 or 200 pips, the line chart will show a point. The line chart is enough to understand the situation if you analyze the trend, i.e., the price direction. But how can we participate in a fast, significant movement if we do not see it even in history? How can we earn from what we cannot see? That is why the candlestick chart is most often used.

In terms of time intervals, charts are divided into:
1M - 5M - one-minute and five-minute charts
15M - 15 minute
30M - half an hour
1H - one hour
4H - 4 hour
D - (daily) daily
W - (weekly) weekly
M is (monthly) monthly

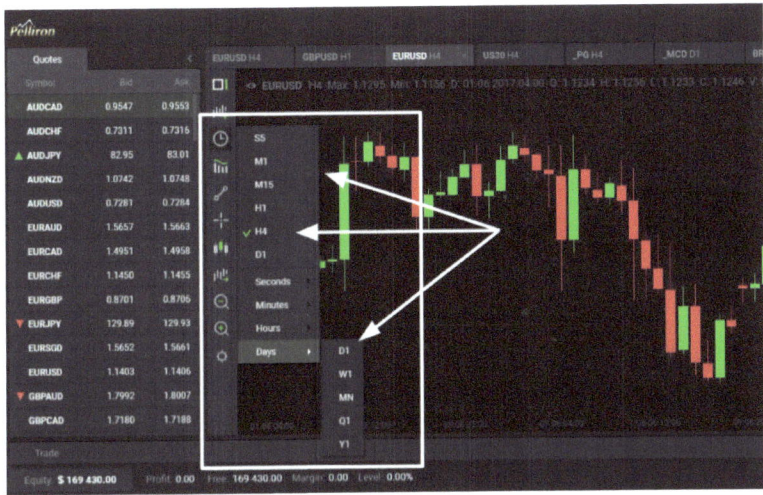

Minute charts are used to identify entry points or for tiny trading strategies, so-called scalping, i.e., trades for the sake of a few pips. A pip is one point movement.
From intraday to 2, 3 days, 1H to 4H charts are used for short-term trading. For medium term - from 5, 7 days to a month, D (daily) is used. W, M charts are used for long-term (strategic) - from several months to a year and more.
The choice of trade type depends on sums of investments, strategy and expected results for the period. Small and medium traders trade short and medium-term more often, depending on their trading strategies. Large traders such as Warren Buffett with Berkshire Hathaway and other investment funds are more likely to trade long-term.
The time intervals on a chart are chart scales. A graph consists of a history of price movements, current price movements and time intervals. Given that technical analysis is based on identifying patterns in price fluctuations, it involves studying current and historical charts.

By observing charts, trends or tendencies are identified.
Prices are constantly moving, as the market is a living organism. Accordingly, prices are always in trend.
Trends are system price fluctuations consisting of tops and bottoms. Prices cannot only rise or fall because any rise or fall stops, at least because participants are unwilling to buy or sell above or below certain price levels.

The second postulate of technical analysis is prices move in trends

By understanding the direction and strength of a trend, traders can make more informed decisions about when to enter or exit a trade. This is often done through the use of charting software and technical indicators that help traders identify trendlines and support and resistance levels.

Beginner traders are not advised to trade against the trend, i.e., if the price rises, you should not sell but rather buy. There is even a saying: "the trend is your friend," meaning you have to go with it, not against it. This is a correct recommendation because if the market goes up, even the heads of states and central banks can not always stop it, not to mention an actual trader.

There is an example of Nick Leeson for this case:

Suppose George Soros is a trader who made much money quickly in the financial markets, trading on the trend. Nick Leeson is a trader who lost a lot in the market; more precisely, he lost England's oldest bank, Barings Bank, which was later sold symbolically for £1. This happened because Leeson went against the market; Nick tried to manipulate the market. He ended up bankrupting the bank. Subsequently, he wrote a book on the subject and began leading seminars on "how you should not act" in the stock market.

Chart 1: Leeson and SIMEX Nikkei futures

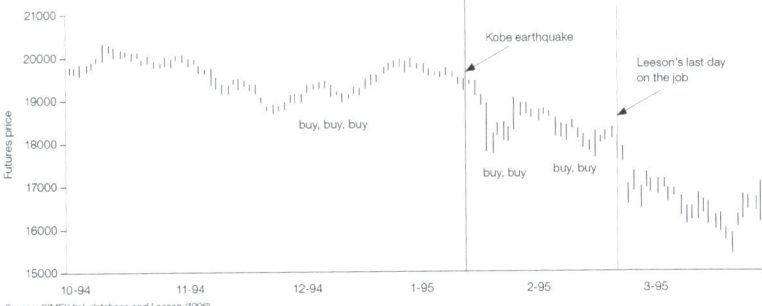

There are three types of trends:

a) An uptrend (uptrend) is a display of price fluctuations during which each successive top is higher than the previous top, and each successive bottom is higher than the previous bottom. It looks like steps upwards.

b) A downtrend is a trend in which each successive bottom is lower than the previous bottom, and each next top is lower than the last top. It looks like downward steps.

c) Lateral trend (flat) - price fluctuations in which each successive top is approximately at the same level as the previous one, and each bottom is also at the level of the previous one. It looks like horizontal fluctuations.

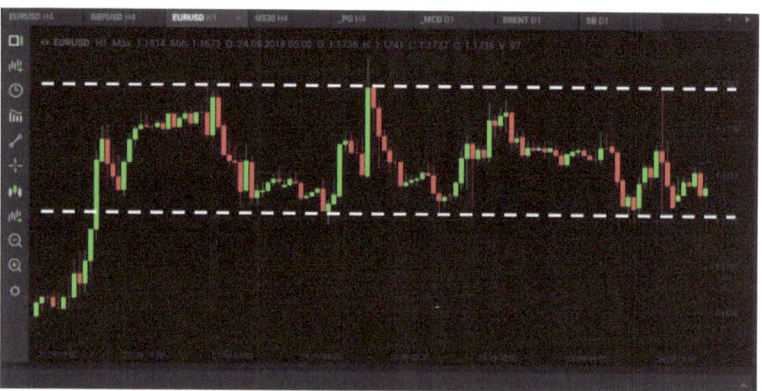

Naturally, each trend is characterized by certain types of transactions.

In an uptrend, prices rise and fall, but they rise much more than they fall. In this type of trend, most traders buy. They buy after small declines, i.e. at prices lower and sell after rising at prices higher. To identify the points of profitable purchases are connected by the line two trend bottoms, so after the next price falls to this line, traders are buying. This line is called the support line (in English - support).

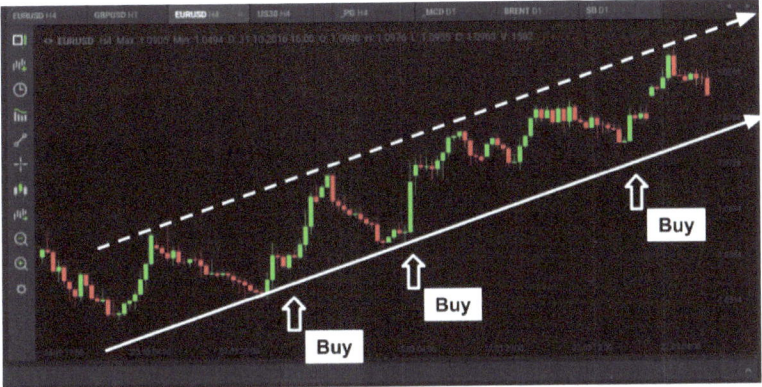

According to trend trading rules, buying from the support line in an uptrend is recommended. And keep the trade open until the resistance line is reached.

The resistance line is the line connecting two trend tops.

The upward movements themselves in an uptrend are called impulses. And periodic weak backward movements, movements against the trend, are called corrections or pullbacks. An impulse is usualy twice as big in volume as a correction and twice as short in time.

Thus, the price rises twice as fast and twice as much as it falls, so a trend is formed, and of course, one should be in a position or buy transaction during these impulses. In that case, the trader earns by buying cheap from support and selling expensive under resistance.

In a downward movement, everything is precisely the opposite. A line, called the resistance line, is drawn through the two tops.

Regardless of trend type, the line above prices is called a resistance line, and the line below prices is called support.

In a downtrend, the resistance line is essential for entering a trade because it is the line from which you should sell high and close transactions (i.e., buy) above the support line.

Buying in a downtrend is not recommended because prices are falling; they fall more and faster than they rise. Those who buy, assume more risks and earn less. Experienced traders who use more complex trading strategies do that. Beginners should adhere to the proverb "trend is your friend" more often, and then they can trade psychologically comfortably and profitably.

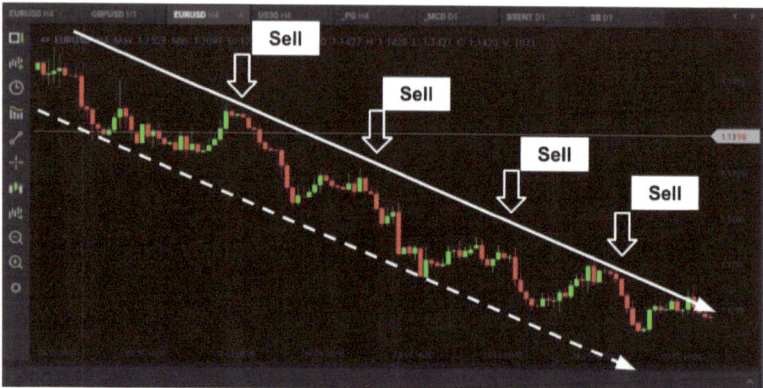

In flat, traders do not trade if the range is too small. However, if the range permits, traders could trade.

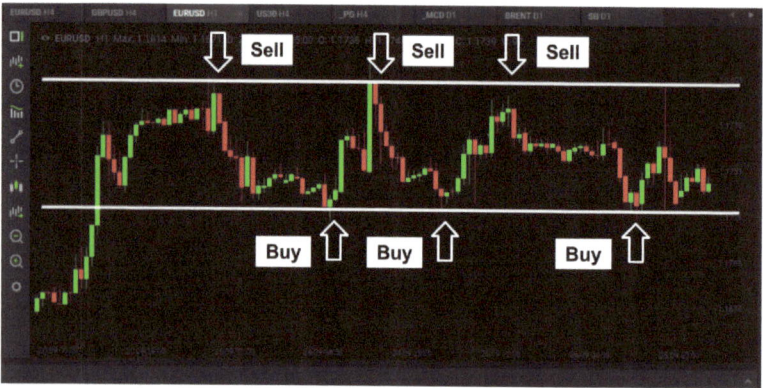

For technical analysis, this is the rule: if we buy, we buy only from support. We buy til the resistance level. The next resistance level is identified from history, as the price has usually already passed through such ranges and also pushed back from the same levels.

The third postulate of technical analysis is that history tends to repeat itself

This means that historical price patterns and trends are likely to continue, and traders can use this information to help predict future price movements. For example, if a currency pair has historically bounced back up from a certain support level, traders may expect it to do so again in the future.

For example:

When the oil price reaches an all-time low or high, or as it recently got a 4-year high, it reverses. Just as it did the last time and the time before. That pattern comes from the expectations and actions of the crowd. Sooner or later, the price will pass that boundary, of course, but it happens less often and is more complex because traders, following this principle, will not buy when it is reached, but on the contrary, they will sell, thus, selling the market. If the price goes up due to fundamental reasons, the growth will slow down at least until the buy trades (longs) are opened again, increasing the prices.

Typically, history repeats itself, and price swings act similarly, perhaps with slight deviations.

History repeats itself. The same is observed in the reverse order. If the price breaks through a support level, it becomes a resistance level, and you can sell from it to the next support level.

The breakdown of a level or line is the closing of one or two candles above or below that level or line, i.e., the closing of a particular time interval and fixation in a new price category.

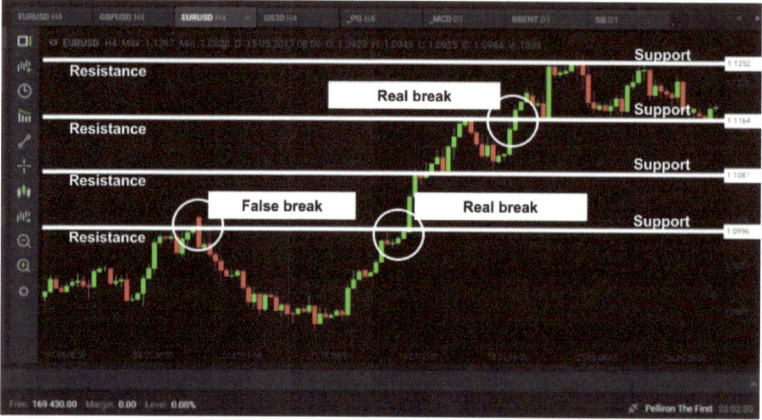

These breakdowns form specific patterns, indicating a certain mood of the market participants. Having studied the patterns it is possible to predict the likely price changes and earn from them, too.

There are numerous pattern types in trading, but here are some of the most common ones:

1. Head and Shoulders Pattern - A reversal pattern that signals a potential shift in trend direction. It is formed by three peaks, with the middle peak (the head) being the highest and the two surrounding peaks (the shoulders) being lower in height.
2. Double Top/Bottom Pattern - A reversal pattern that occurs after an extended uptrend or downtrend. It is characterized by two peaks or valleys that are roughly the same height, separated by a temporary price retracement.
3. Ascending/Descending Triangle Pattern - A continuation pattern that indicates a potential continuation of an existing trend. An ascending triangle is formed by a horizontal resistance line and an upward sloping support line, while a descending triangle is formed by a horizontal support line and a downward sloping resistance line.
4. Bullish/Bearish Flag Pattern - A continuation pattern that signals a temporary pause in an existing trend before resuming its original direction. A bullish flag is formed by a price rally followed by a brief consolidation period, while a bearish flag is formed by a price decline followed by a brief consolidation period.
5. Pennant Pattern - A continuation pattern that looks similar to a triangle pattern, but with converging trendlines. It indicates a temporary consolidation before the continuation of the original trend.
6. Candlestick Patterns - Candlesticks represent the open, high, low, and close of a given time period. Different candlestick patterns can indicate different market conditions and can be used in combination with other technical analysis tools.

Few of them you can see here, but detailed learning of their use will be at the "Intermediate trading course" workshops.

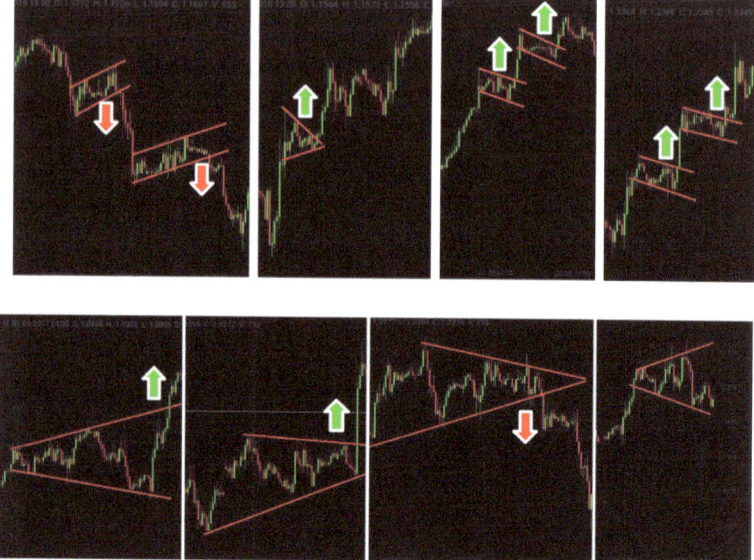

While technical analysis can be a valuable tool for traders, it's important to note that it is not foolproof. Market conditions can change rapidly, and historical patterns may not always accurately predict future price movements. As such, it's important for traders to use technical analysis in combination with other approaches, such as fundamental analysis and risk management strategies, to make informed trading decisions.

Overall, technical analysis is an important tool that traders, especially forex traders, can use to gain insights into historical price patterns and trends. By understanding the three main postulates of technical analysis, traders can make more informed decisions about when to enter or exit a trade, and can better anticipate potential future price movements in the forex market.

Risk and money management

In addition to fundamental and technical analysis, effective risk and money management is a critical component of successful forex trading. Risk management involves identifying potential risks and taking steps to minimize them, while money management involves making decisions about how much capital to allocate to each trade and how to manage that capital over time.

One key aspect of risk management in forex trading is understanding the concept of leverage. Leverage allows traders to control a larger position than their account balance would otherwise allow, but it also increases the risk of loss. As such, traders must be careful to manage their leverage effectively and ensure that they are not overexposed to the market.

Another important aspect of risk management is setting appropriate stop-loss and take-profit levels. Stop-loss levels are predetermined points at which a trade will be automatically closed if the market moves against the trader, while take-profit levels are predetermined points at which a trade will be automatically closed if the market moves in the trader's favor. By setting appropriate stop-loss and take-profit levels, traders can limit their potential losses and lock in profits.

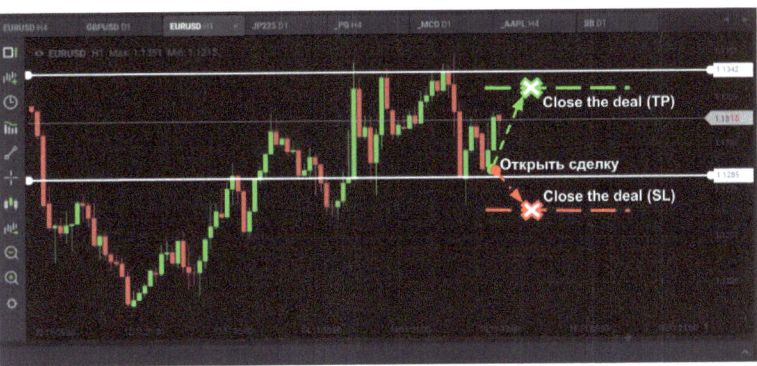

Here are some common stop loss and take profit rules that traders follow:

1. Use technical analysis: Forex traders often use technical analysis to identify key support and resistance levels, set their stop loss and take profit levels accordingly. For instance, a stop loss might be placed just below a key support level, while a take profit level might be placed just below a key resistance level.
2. Consider volatility: Traders should consider the volatility of the currency pair they are trading when setting their stop loss and take profit levels. More volatile currency pairs may require wider stop loss and take profit levels, while less volatile pairs may require narrower levels.
3. Set realistic levels: Traders need to set stop loss and take profit levels that are realistic and achievable based on market conditions. Setting levels too tight may result in premature stop outs, while setting levels too wide may result in missed opportunities for profit.

4. **Adjust levels as needed:** Traders should be ready to adjust their stop loss and take profit levels as market conditions change. For instance, if a trade is moving in the trader's favor, they may choose to move their stop loss level to break even or even into profit territory.

Overall, stop loss and take profit rules are essential tools for managing risk and maximising profitability in forex trading. By using technical analysis, considering volatility, setting realistic levels, and adjusting levels as needed, traders can increase their chances of success in the market.

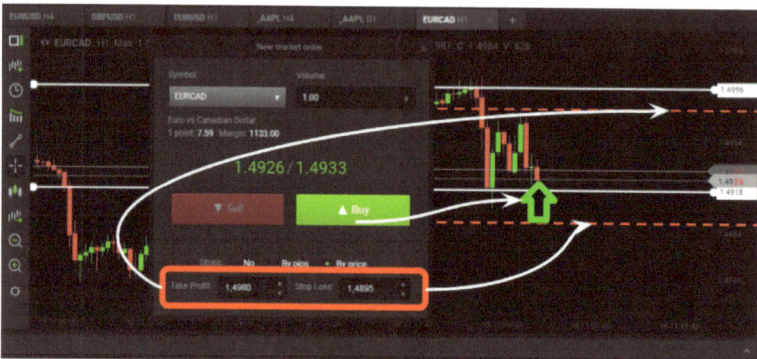

When opening a buy trade, the trade opens from support, stop loss is placed under support, take profit is placed under resistance. When opening a sell trade - the trade opens under resistance, stop loss is placed over resistance, take profit over support.

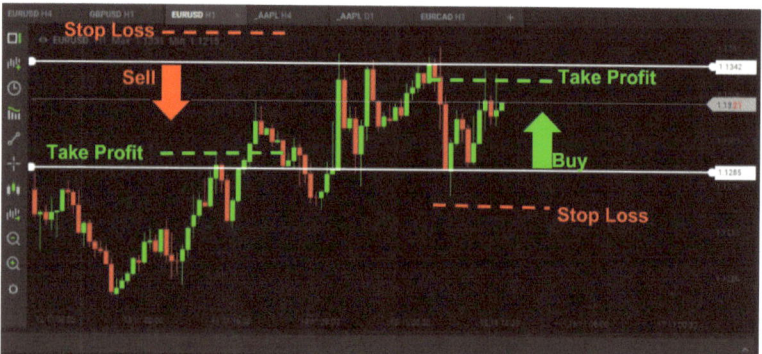

Closing deal calculations

The expected profit should always be greater than the expected risks. Otherwise, it is not a business and not even a charity.

In this case, the Take Profit should be greater than the Stop Loss (TP > SL).

But how much more?

The more - the better! Desirable for many traders is 3:1, but for this, you have to be at the monitor very often and watch or miss many good opportunities with more minor but still profitable. It is often possible to use 2:1, which is also good. And 1.5:1 is also good. After all, the profit is greater... At the very least, it is possible to use 1:1 from mathematical calculations, if you haven't earned, at least you haven't lost anything!

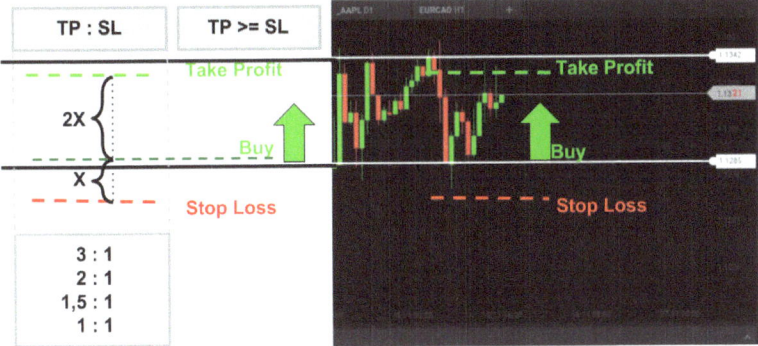

Money management is also a critical component of successful forex trading. This involves making decisions about how much capital to allocate to each trade and how to manage that capital over time. One common approach is to use a fixed percentage of account equity as the maximum risk per trade, typically 1-2%. This helps traders avoid overexposing themselves to the market and ensures that they have sufficient capital to continue trading over the long term.

Another key aspect of money management is understanding the importance of diversification. By spreading their capital across multiple currency pairs, traders can minimize their exposure to any one particular market and reduce their overall risk. Additionally, traders should be prepared to adjust their capital allocation over time as market conditions change.

In addition to fundamental and technical analysis, as well as effective risk and money management, there are several common rules that traders can follow to increase the rate of profitable deals in the forex market. Here are some of the most important ones:

1. Stick to a trading plan: Traders should develop a clear and well-defined trading plan that outlines their strategies, goals, and risk management techniques. By sticking to this plan, traders can avoid making impulsive decisions and ensure that they are consistently following a well-thought-out approach to trading.
2. Be patient: Forex trading requires patience and discipline. Traders should avoid the temptation to make impulsive trades based on short-term market movements and instead focus on long-term trends and patterns.
3. Learn from mistakes: Every trader will make mistakes, but the most successful traders are those who learn from those mistakes and use them to improve their strategies and decision-making processes.
4. Keep emotions in check: Forex trading can be emotionally challenging, but successful traders know how to keep their emotions in check and avoid making impulsive decisions based on fear, greed, or other emotional responses.
5. Stay informed: Traders should stay up to date on market news and developments, as well as changes in economic policies and indicators, to make informed trading decisions.
6. Use a variety of strategies: Successful traders often use a combination of fundamental and technical analysis, as well as a range of trading strategies, to achieve their goals. By diversifying their approach, traders can take advantage of a wider range of market conditions and increase their chances of profitability.

By following these common rules, forex traders can increase their chances of success in the market and achieve their goals over the long term.

In summary, effective risk and money management is a critical component of successful forex trading. By understanding the concept of leverage, setting appropriate stop-loss and take-profit levels, and making smart decisions about how to allocate and manage their capital, forex traders can minimise their risk and maximise their potential for long-term profitability in the market.
Here are the meanings of four trading techniques that traders may use in the forex market:

1. Reversing position: This technique involves closing out an existing position and then opening a new position in the opposite direction. Traders may use

this technique if they believe that the market is about to change direction or if their original trade is no longer profitable.

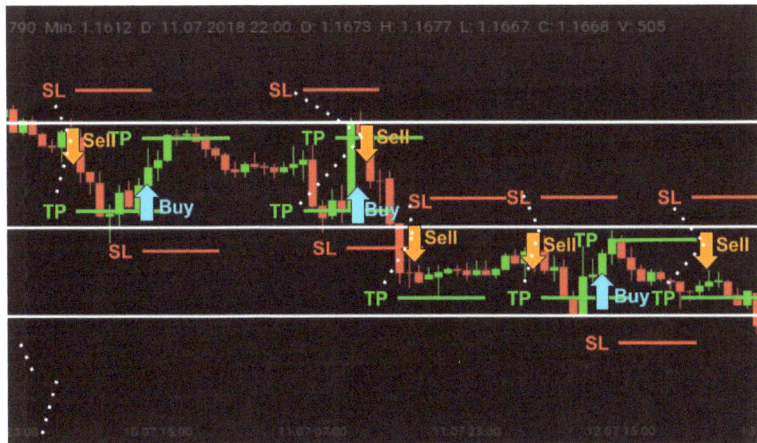

2. Lock: Locking is a technique that involves opening a second position in the opposite direction of an existing position, to minimise losses if the market moves against the original position. This technique is also known as hedging.

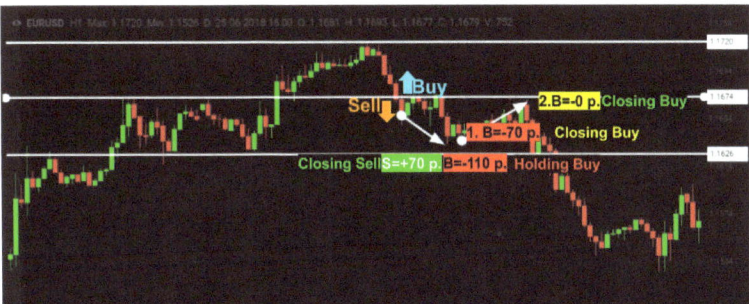

3. Adding to loss position: This technique involves increasing the size of an existing losing position in the hope that the market will eventually move in the trader's favor. This technique can be risky and requires careful risk management, as it can lead to larger losses if the market continues to move against the position.

4. Adding to profitable position: This technique involves increasing the size of an existing profitable position in the hope of making even greater profits. Traders who use this technique may do so if they have a strong conviction that the market will continue to move in their favor. However, like adding to a losing position, this technique requires careful risk management to avoid large losses if the market moves against the position.

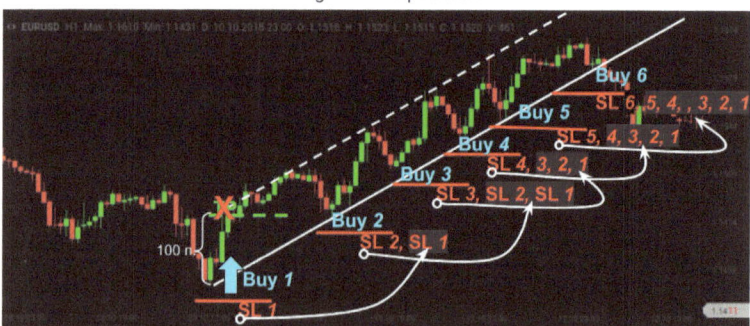

There are many different types of trading strategies that traders use in the forex market, each with its strengths and weaknesses. Here are some common types of trading strategies:

1. Trend following: Trend following is a strategy that involves identifying the direction of the market's trend and then making trades in that direction. Traders who use this strategy may use technical analysis to identify trends, such as moving averages or trend lines.

2. Breakout: A breakout strategy involves identifying key levels of support and resistance and making trades when the market breaks through these levels. Traders who use this strategy may use technical analysis to identify key levels, such as pivot points or price channels.
3. Range trading: Range trading involves identifying a range-bound market, where the price is moving within a certain range, and making trades based on this range. Traders who use this strategy may use technical analysis to identify the range, such as using support and resistance levels.
4. News trading: News trading involves making trades based on upcoming economic news releases, such as interest rate announcements or employment data. Traders who use this strategy may use fundamental analysis to identify which news releases are likely to have an impact on the market.
5. Position trading: Position trading involves holding trades for a longer time, such as weeks or months, and making trades based on long-term trends or fundamentals. Traders who use this strategy may use a combination of technical and fundamental analysis to identify longer-term trends.
6. Scalping: Scalping is a high-frequency trading strategy that involves making many trades in a short time to capture small profits. Traders who use this strategy may use technical analysis to identify short-term price movements.

All these we will learn at the "Intermediate trading course" workshops, which should continue after you finish reading the book.

Conclusion

As we come to the end of this Beginner's Financial Markets Trading Guide, I hope you have gained valuable insights into the world of trading and investment. You have learned about the different types of financial markets, how to analyse them, and how to manage risk. You now understand the importance of creating a trading plan and sticking to it, and how to use technical and fundamental analysis to make informed trading decisions.

But this is only the beginning. The world of trading is constantly evolving, and there is always more to learn. That's why I am excited to announce that TradersTime, one of the leading trading companies, is offering an intermediate trading course that builds on the concepts covered in this book.

This course consists of practical workshops where you will learn from experienced traders and get hands-on experience in trading. And the best part? I will be there to teach you personally, helping you to refine your skills and take your trading to the next level.

If you are serious about trading and want to continue your education, then I encourage you to enrol in TradersTime's intermediate trading course. Together, we can help you achieve your financial goals and become a successful trader. Thank you for joining me on this journey, and I look forward to seeing you in the next course! The intermediate trading course at TradersTime is designed to help traders build on their existing knowledge and take their trading to the next level. Here is a brief outline of what you can expect to learn in the course:

1. Advanced Technical Analysis: In this module, you will learn advanced charting techniques, including different types of charts, candlestick patterns, and technical indicators. You will also learn how to use these tools to identify trends, spot trading opportunities, and manage risk.
2. Fundamental Analysis: In this module, you will learn how to analyze economic data, company financial statements, and other fundamental factors that can impact the markets. You will also learn how to use this information to make informed trading decisions.
3. Risk Management: In this module, you will learn advanced risk management techniques, including position sizing, stop-loss orders, and other strategies to limit your losses and maximize your profits.
4. Trading Psychology: In this module, you will learn how to develop the right mindset for successful trading, including how to overcome common trading mistakes, deal with emotions, and maintain discipline.
5. Trading Strategies: In this module, you will learn about different trading strategies, including day trading, swing trading, and position trading. You will also learn how to develop your trading strategy based on your personality, goals, and risk tolerance.

Throughout the course, you will have the opportunity to apply your learning in practical workshops, where you will trade under the guidance of experienced traders. You will also receive personalized feedback and coaching from the course instructors, including myself, to help you refine your skills and become a successful trader.

A crucial component of successful trading is having a solid business plan that covers trading planning, financial planning, and action planning. Here's how the TradersTime intermediate trading course will help you develop and implement a comprehensive business plan for your trading activities:

1. Trading Planning: You will learn how to create a trading plan that outlines your goals, trading style, risk tolerance, and the markets and instruments you will

trade. You will also learn how to develop a trading strategy that aligns with your plan and how to use technical and fundamental analysis to identify trading opportunities. The course will teach you how to refine your plan over time to adapt to changing market conditions and improve your results.
2. Financial Planning: You will learn how to create a financial plan that takes into account your trading goals, income, expenses, and risk management strategies. You will learn how to calculate your risk and reward potential, set realistic profit targets, and manage your trading capital effectively. The course will also teach you how to monitor your performance and adjust your financial plan as needed to stay on track.
3. Action Planning: You will learn how to create an action plan that outlines the steps you will take to implement your trading and financial plans. This will include setting up your trading platform, selecting your trading tools, and establishing your trading routine. You will also learn how to track your progress and make adjustments to your plan as needed.

By the end of the course, you will have a comprehensive business plan for your trading activities that will help you stay focused, disciplined, and consistent in your approach. You will have the tools and knowledge you need to manage your risk, maximize your profits, and achieve your financial goals.

QUIZ

1. What is the forex market?

A. A market where companies go public and raise capital
B. A market where investors buy and sell stocks and bonds
C. A market where currencies are traded

2. What is a currency pair?

A. A pair of highly correlated stocks
B. A pair of bonds with similar yields
C. A pair of currencies that are traded together

3. What is a pip in forex trading?

A. The smallest unit of a currency pair
B. The difference between the bid and ask price
C. The amount of leverage used in a trade

4. What is a bid/ask spread?

A. The difference between the price at which a trader can buy and sell a currency pair
B. The difference between the price at which a trader can buy and the price at which a trader can sell a stock

C. The difference between the price at which a trader can buy and the price at which a trader can sell a commodity

5. What is a lot in forex trading?
A. The amount of currency being traded
B. The difference between the bid and ask price
C. The amount of leverage used in a trade

6. What is leverage in forex trading?
A. A way to reduce risk by diversifying investments
B. A way to increase potential returns by borrowing money to invest
C. A way to minimize losses by setting stop-loss orders
D. A way to trade on margin with a broker

7. What is a stop-loss order in forex trading?
A. An order to buy or sell a currency pair at a specific price
B. An order to buy or sell a currency pair at the current market price
C. An order to close a trade when a certain level of loss is reached
D. An order to close a trade when a certain level of profit is reached

8. What is a carry trade in forex trading?
A. A strategy where a trader borrows money in a low-interest-rate currency and invests it in a high-interest-rate currency
B. A strategy where a trader buys and holds a currency for a long time
C. A strategy where a trader buys and sells a currency pair rapidly to capture small price movements

9. What is a fundamental analysis in forex trading?
A. Analysis of a currency pair's chart patterns and trends
B. Analysis of a country's economic and political factors that may impact the currency's value
C. Analysis of market psychology and sentiment

10. What is technical analysis in forex trading?
A. Analysis of a currency pair's chart patterns and trends
B. Analysis of a country's economic and political factors that may impact the currency's value
C. Analysis of market psychology and sentiment

Answers:

1. C

2. C
3. A
4. A
5. A
6. B
7. C
8. A
9. B
10. A

Congratulations on finishing the Beginner's Financial Markets Trading Guide quiz! You've taken an important first step towards developing your skills as a trader. If you found the quiz challenging, don't worry - the more you practice, the better you'll become.

To take your trading skills to the next level, we invite you to consider joining our intermediate trading course. This course will provide you with practical workshops and personalized instruction from our team of experienced traders. You'll learn valuable skills such as trading planning, financial planning, and action planning, and gain hands-on experience in trading in the forex market and other financial markets.

As the author of the Beginner's Financial Markets Trading Guide, I will be directly involved in teaching the intermediate course. I'm excited to share my knowledge and experience with you and help you take your trading to the next level.

Don't miss this opportunity to learn from the best - enroll in our intermediate trading course today!

https://www.traderstime.co.uk/

www.ingramcontent.com/pod-product-compliance
Lightning Source LLC
Chambersburg PA
CBHW040238220526
45473CB00001B/289